亚当夏娃日记

Diaries of Adam and Eve

〔美国〕马克·吐温 著
徐彬　张怡青 译

译林出版社

目 录

亚当日记 001

夏娃日记 079

亚当日记续 167

夏娃日记续 183

亚当日记

星期一

这个长头发的新生物真碍事。它总是在我周围晃悠，跟着我走来走去。我不喜欢这样，也不习惯有谁陪在我身边。我希望它老老实实地和其他动物待在一起。今天阴天，刮东风，感觉我们要有雨了……我们？这个词，我是从哪儿学来的？对，想起来了——是新生物用的。

Monday

This new creature with the long hair is a good deal in the way. It is always hanging around and following me about. I don't like this; I am not used to company. I wish it would stay with the other animals. Cloudy today, wind in the east; think we shall have rain.... Where did I get that word? ... I remember now—the new creature uses it.

星期二

我仔细地观察了大瀑布。我觉得大瀑布是这里最美的事物。新来的人为其取名为尼亚加拉大瀑布——我不知道这个名字是怎么取的。新来的人说因为它看起来像尼亚加拉大瀑布。

Tuesday

Been examining the great waterfall. It is the finest thing on the estate, I think. The new creature calls it Niagara Falls—why, I am sure I do not know. Says it looks like Niagara Falls.

这可不是理由，仅仅是因为任性和愚蠢罢了。我根本没有机会为事物取名。我还来不及提出抗议，新来的人就为所有遇到的东西取好了名字。每次的理由都一样——那东西看起来像什么，就取了那个名。

That is not a reason; it is mere waywardness and imbecility. I get no chance to name anything myself. The new creature names everything that comes along, before I can get in a protest. And always that same pretext is offered—it looks like the thing.

比如渡渡鸟，新来的人说只要看上一眼，就会觉得那东西“看起来像渡渡鸟”。毫无疑问，渡渡鸟这个名字就定下来了。我厌烦自己为这件事苦恼，而且这样做又没好处。渡渡鸟！那东西看起来像渡渡鸟？我看还不如我像呢。

There is the dodo, for instance. Says the moment one looks at it one sees at a glance that it “looks like a dodo.” It will have to keep that name, no doubt. It wearies me to fret about it, and it does no good, anyway. Dodo! It looks no more like a dodo than I do.

星期三

我搭了个避雨的居所，却不能静静地独自享用。新来的生物闯了进来。当我把它赶出去的时候，它那用来看东西的两个小孔流出了水，然后它用它爪子的背面把水擦去，还发出动物伤心时会发出的声音。

Wednesday

Built me a shelter against the rain, but could not have it to myself in peace. The new creature intruded. When I tried to put it out it shed water out of the holes it looks with, and wiped it away with the back of its paws, and made a noise such as some of the other animals make when they are in distress.

它总是在说话，我希望它能消停一会儿。这听起来像是对这个可怜的东西的嘲讽，是在诽谤它，但我本意并非如此。我只是从未听过人的声音，这片梦一般孤寂的地方庄严静谧，任何新奇的声音都会让我的耳朵不舒服，听着不对劲。而且新来的人的声音离我太近了；就在我的肩头，在我耳边，先是在这一侧，然后又到了另一侧，而我所习惯的声音，多少都离我比较远一些。

I wish it would not talk; it is always talking. That sounds like a cheap fling at the poor creature, a slur; but I do not mean it so. I have never heard the human voice before, and any new and strange sound intruding itself here upon the solemn hush of these dreaming solitudes offends my ear and seems a false note. And this new sound is so close to me; it is right at my shoulder, right at my ear, first on one side and then on the other, and I am used only to sounds that are more or less distant from me.

星期五

虽然能做的我都做了，但新生物仍在无所顾忌地取名。对于这个地方，我本来有个特别好的名字，动听又美丽，叫作“伊甸园”。私下里，我还是用这个称呼，但公开使用就不行了。因为它说这里全是树木、岩石和自然风光，所以一点也不像花园。它还说这里像个公园，别的什么也不像。

Friday

The naming goes recklessly on, in spite of anything I can do. I had a very good name for the estate, and it was musical and pretty—GARDEN-OF-EDEN. Privately, I continue to call it that, but not any longer publicly. The new creature says it is all woods and rocks and scenery, and therefore has no resemblance to a garden. Says it looks like a park, and does not look like anything but a park.

结果，在没跟我商量的情况下，这地方就有了一个新名字——尼亚加拉瀑布公园。在我看来，这种行为真是专横得很。而且它还立了一块标识牌，上面写着：

不要践踏草地！

我的日子没有之前快乐了。

Consequently, without consulting me, it has been new-named—NIAGARA FALLS PARK. This is sufficiently high-handed, it seems to me. And already there is a sign up:

KEEP OFF THE GRASS

My life is not as happy as it was.

星期六

新生物吃了太多果子。我们很可能要遇到水果短缺的情况了。我又用了“我们”——这个词是新生物用的，我现在也用这个词了。今天早上雾很大。有雾的话，我不会独自出门。但新生物照样会出去。无论什么天气，它都会出门，哪怕回来的时候脚上沾满泥巴，也直接迈步就进来。新生物总在说话。之前这里可是又宜人又安静的。

Saturday

The new creature eats too much fruit. We are going to run short, most likely. “We” again—that is its word; mine too, now, from hearing it so much. Good deal of fog this morning. I do not go out in the fog myself. The new creature does. It goes out in all weathers, and stumps right in with its muddy feet. And talks. It used to be so pleasant and quiet here.

星期天

熬过一日。星期天越来越难熬。去年十一月，这一天被挑出来专门作为休息日。但在这天之前，我每个星期已经有六天休息的日子了。今天上午，我发现这个新生物在试图用土块把禁树上的苹果打下来。

Sunday

Pulled through. This day is getting to be more and more trying. It was selected and set apart last November as a day of rest. I already had six of them per week, before. This morning [I] found the new creature trying to clod apples out of that forbidden tree.

星期一

新生物说它的名字叫夏娃。这没问题，我并不反对。它说我可以在找它的时候喊这个名字。当时，我说这纯属多余。但“多余”这个词，显然让它对我更加尊敬；这的确是个很大、很好的词，经得起多说几遍。新生物还说它不是“它”，而是“她”。我对此怀有疑问；但无论如何它对我来说都是同一个生物。只要她安安静静地自己待着，不要说话，她究竟是什么，对我而言无关紧要。

Monday

The new creature says its name is Eve. That is all right, I have no objections. Says it is to call it by when I want it to come. I said it was superfluous, then. The word evidently raised me in its respect; and indeed it is a large, good word, and will bear repetition. It says it is not an It, it is a She. This is probably doubtful; yet it is all one to me; what she is were nothing to me if she would but go by herself and not talk.

星期二

她用讨人厌的名字和标识牌把这个地方弄得一团乱，牌子上写着：

> 此路通往漩涡。
>
> 此路通往山羊岛。
>
> 风洞由此向前。

Tuesday

She has littered the whole estate with execrable names and offensive signs:

> THIS WAY TO THE WHIRLPOOL.
>
> THIS WAY TO GOAT ISLAND.
>
> CAVE OF THE WINDS THIS WAY.

她说这里会变成一个不错的避暑胜地，如果有这种做法的话。避暑胜地——这是她发明的另一个词——只是词语而已，没有任何意义。不过，什么是避暑胜地呢？最好别问她，否则她会解释个没完没了。

She says this park would make a tidy summer resort, if there was any custom for it. Summer resort—another invention of hers—just words, without any meaning. What is a summer resort? But it is best not to ask her, she has such a rage for explaining.

星期五

她最近总是求我不要再去瀑布了。去瀑布那边有什么坏处吗？她说那会让她不寒而栗。我不明白为什么。我总是这么做——我喜欢水流直泻而下，喜欢那种凉爽。我认为这正是瀑布的作用。我看不出它们还有什么别的用处，而且它们一定是为了有些什么用处才存在的。她说瀑布的存在只是为了风景而已——就像犀牛和乳齿象一样。

Friday

She has taken to beseeching me to stop going over the Falls. What harm does it do? Says it makes her shudder. I wonder why. I have always done it—always liked the plunge, and the excitement, and the coolness. I supposed it was what the Falls were for. They have no other use that I can see, and they must have been made for something. She says they were only made for scenery—like the rhinoceros and the mastodon.

我坐着木桶前往瀑布——但她不满意。我坐着盆去——她还是不满意。我穿着无花果叶子做的衣服，到漩涡和急流中游泳。结果衣服破损得很厉害。于是她又没完没了地抱怨我浪费。我在这里真是束手束脚。我必须要换个地方了。

I went over the Falls in a barrel—not satisfactory to her. Went over in a tub—still not satisfactory. Swam the Whirlpool and the Rapids in a fig-leaf suit. It got much damaged. Hence, tedious complaints about my extravagance. I am too much hampered here. What I need is change of scene.

星期六

上周二的晚上，我逃出来游荡了两天，在隐蔽的地方造了另一个住处，还尽可能把我的踪迹掩盖起来，但她还是凭借一头由她驯服的野兽找到了我，她把那头野兽叫作狼，她又发出了那种可怜的声音，用来看东西的地方也流出水来。我只好跟她回去，但只要时机一到，我还是会立刻离开。

Saturday

I escaped last Tuesday night, and travelled two days, and built me another shelter, in a secluded place, and obliterated my tracks as well as I could, but she hunted me out by means of a beast which she has tamed and calls a wolf, and came making that pitiful noise again, and shedding that water out of the places she looks with. I was obliged to return with her, but will presently emigrate again, when occasion offers.

她做了许多愚蠢的事——比如，她想知道为什么叫作狮子和老虎的动物会以草和花为生，据她所说，从它们所拥有的锋利牙齿来看，它们应该相互撕咬、吃掉对方。这太蠢了，因为这样做就会杀死对方，就会招来我理解的所谓的“死亡”；而据我所知，这个地方从未发生过死亡。从某些方面来说，我觉得这有点遗憾。

She engages herself in many foolish things: among others, trying to study out why the animals called lions and tigers live on grass and flowers, when, as she says, the sort of teeth they wear would indicate that they were intended to eat each other. This is foolish, because to do that would be to kill each other, and that would introduce what, as I understand it, is called “death”; and death, as I have been told, has not yet entered the Park. Which is a pity, on some accounts.

星期天

熬过一日。

Sunday

Pulled through.

星期一

我相信我明白了每个星期的意义：它是为了消除星期天的疲劳。这个主意似乎不错…… 她又爬上了那棵树。我用土块把她赶了下来。她说反正没人在看。她似乎认为只要没人看见，就有充分的正当理由去冒险。我把这话告诉了她。“正当理由”这个词让她十分赞赏——我想她或许还有点妒忌。这真是个好词。

Monday

I believe I see what the week is for: it is to give time to rest up from the weariness of Sunday. It seems a good idea.... She has been climbing that tree again. Clodded her out of it. She said nobody was looking. Seems to consider that a sufficient justification for chancing any dangerous thing. Told her that. The word justification moved her admiration—and envy too, I thought. It is a good word.

星期四

她告诉我，她是用我身上的一根肋骨做的。就算这不是胡说，多少也让人怀疑。我明明没有缺少肋骨…… 她很为那只秃鹫操心：她觉得秃鹫应该吃腐肉而不是青草，她担心养不了它。我觉得，秃鹫应该尽可能地适应现有情况。我们不能为了迁就秃鹫，而推翻所有的秩序。

Thursday

She told me she was made out of a rib taken from my body. This is at least doubtful, if not more than that. I have not missed any rib.... She is in much trouble about the buzzard; says grass does not agree with it, is afraid she can't raise it; thinks it was intended to live on decayed flesh. The buzzard must get along the best it can with what is provided. We cannot overturn the whole scheme to accommodate the buzzard.

星期六

她常常在池塘边看自己的倒影，昨天她又这样做，结果掉下去了。她差点窒息而死，她说那种差点窒息的感觉让她很难受。

Saturday

She fell in the pond yesterday, when she was looking at herself in it, which she is always doing. She nearly strangled, and said it was most uncomfortable.

于是她很同情活在水里的生物，她把它们叫作“鱼”——她仍然在给各种东西取名，其实它们并不需要名字，就算喊那些名字它们也不会来，不过这对她无关紧要，反正她就是这么傻——昨天晚上她把鱼捞出来，放在我的床上让它们取暖。然而，我整天不时去看看这些鱼，也没看出它们比以前更快乐，只是更安静了。

This made her sorry for the creatures which live in there, which she calls fish, for she continues to fasten names on to things that don't need them and don't come when they are called by them, which is a matter of no consequence to her, as she is such a numskull anyway; so she got a lot of them out and brought them in last night and put them in my bed to keep warm, but I have noticed them now and then all day, and I don't see that they are any happier there than they were before, only quieter.

等夜幕降临，我就要把它们扔出去。我不想再和鱼一起睡觉，因为我发现，如果光着身子和它们躺在一起，就会又湿又冷，很不舒服。

When night comes I shall throw them out-doors. I will not sleep with them again, for I find them clammy and unpleasant to lie among when a person hasn't anything on.

星期天

熬过一日。

Sunday

Pulled through.

星期二

她现在和一条蛇关系很好。其他动物都很高兴，因为她总是拿它们做实验，打扰它们；我也很高兴，因为蛇会说话，我就能休息一下了。

Tuesday

She has taken up with a snake now. The other animals are glad, for she was always experimenting with them and bothering them; and I am glad, because the snake talks, and this enables me to get a rest.

星期五

她说，蛇建议她尝尝那棵树的果子，结果会是一次重要、美好而又高尚的教育。我告诉她，还会有另一种结果——这样做会把死亡带到这个世界。我不该指出这一点的——把这话放在心里会更好；我这样说，只会让她想到，她可以拯救生病的秃鹫，也能给垂头丧气的狮子和老虎提供新鲜的肉。我劝她不要靠近那棵树。她说她不会靠近的。我觉得要有麻烦。我要离开这里。

Friday

She says the snake advises her to try the fruit of that tree, and says the result will be a great and fine and noble education. I told her there would be another result, too—it would introduce death into the world. That was a mistake—it had been better to keep the remark to myself; it only gave her an idea—she could save the sick buzzard, and furnish fresh meat to the despondent lions and tigers. I advised her to keep away from the tree. She said she wouldn't. I foresee trouble. Will emigrate.

星期三

我过得很愉快。昨晚我逃了出来，骑了一整夜的马，尽可能地快跑，希望能在麻烦发生之前离开公园，躲到别的地方去；但我没能如愿。

Wednesday

I have had a variegated time. I escaped that night, and rode a horse all night as fast as he could go, hoping to get clear out of the Park and hide in some other country before the trouble should begin; but it was not to be.

日出后大约一小时，我骑着马穿过一片鲜花盛开的平原，数不清的动物正如往常一样各随其好地吃草、睡觉或相互嬉戏，突然，它们发出一阵暴风雨般可怕的声音，一时间，整个平原陷入了疯狂的骚动中，每一只野兽都在撕咬身边的同伴。

About an hour after sunup, as I was riding through a flowery plain where thousands of animals were grazing, slumbering, or playing with each other, according to their wont, all of a sudden they broke into a tempest of frightful noises, and in one moment the plain was in a frantic commotion and every beast was destroying its neighbor.

我知道这是怎么回事——夏娃吃了那棵禁树的果子，死亡来到了这个世界……老虎吃了我的马，当我让它们不要那样做，它们毫不理睬。如果我留下来，它们也会把我吃掉的——我没有留下，而是匆忙地离开了……我找到了现在这个地方，在公园外面，这几天相当舒服，但她还是找到了我。

I knew what it meant—Eve had eaten that fruit, and death was come into the world.... The tigers ate my horse, paying no attention when I ordered them to desist, and they would even have eaten me if I had stayed—which I didn't, but went away in much haste.... I found this place, outside the Park, and was fairly comfortable for a few days, but she has found me out.

她找了过来，还把这个地方命名为“托那旺达”——说它看起来像“托那旺达”。事实上，我并不觉得她的到来不好，因为这里能摘的东西很少，而她带来了一些苹果。我太饿了，不得不吃了些苹果。这有违我的原则，但我发现，在填不饱肚子的时候，原则是虚弱无力的……

Found me out, and has named the place Tonawanda—says it looks like that. In fact, I was not sorry she came, for there are but meagre pickings here, and she brought some of those apples. I was obliged to eat them, I was so hungry. It was against my principles, but I find that principles have no real force except when one is well fed....

她来的时候，身上的树枝和一把把树叶像帘子一样遮蔽着她的身体，我问她这样瞎闹是什么意思，还把枝叶一把拽下来扔到了地上，这时她傻傻地笑了，脸涨得通红。我从来没有见过一个人这样哧哧地傻笑、脸红，在我看来，这既难看又愚蠢。她说我很快就会知道怎么回事。这话说得对。

She came curtained in boughs and bunches of leaves, and when I asked her what she meant by such nonsense, and snatched them away and threw them down, she tittered and blushed. I had never seen a person titter and blush before, and to me it seemed unbecoming and idiotic. She said I would soon know how it was myself. This was correct.

虽然我很饿，但苹果只吃了一半我就放下了——虽然这无疑是我所见过的最好的苹果，毕竟这个季节就要过去了——我把刚才扔掉的树枝挂在自己身上，然后有些严肃地跟她说话，让她再去找些树枝来，不要这样出洋相。

Hungry as I was, I laid down the apple half eaten—certainly the best one I ever saw, considering the lateness of the season—and arrayed myself in the discarded boughs and branches, and then spoke to her with some severity and ordered her to go and get some more and not make such a spectacle of herself.

夏娃照做了，之后，我们爬到野兽搏斗过的地方，收集了一些兽皮，我让她做了几件在公开场合穿的衣服。这些衣服的确不舒服，但很时尚，时尚才是衣服的重点……

She did it, and after this we crept down to where the wild-beast battle had been, and collected some skins, and I made her patch together a couple of suits proper for public occasions. They are uncomfortable, it is true, but stylish, and that is the main point about clothes....

我发现她是个很好的伴侣。我明白，我已经失去了所有的一切，如果再没有她，我会感到寂寞和沮丧。还有一件事，她说今后我们必须干活来养活自己，她也会帮忙。我会监督她的。

I find she is a good deal of a companion. I see I should be lonesome and depressed without her, now that I have lost my property. Another thing, she says it is ordered that we work for our living hereafter. She will be useful. I will superintend.

十天后

她竟然指责我，说我是造成这场灾难的原因！她带着一脸恳切和真诚说，那条蛇曾向她保证，禁果不是苹果，而是栗子。我说我是无辜的，因为我没有吃过什么栗子。她说，蛇告诉她，“栗子”是个比喻的说法，指的是老掉牙的过时笑话。

Ten Days Later

She accuses me of being the cause of our disaster! She says, with apparent sincerity and truth, that the Serpent assured her that the forbidden fruit was not apples, it was chestnuts. I said I was innocent, then, for I had not eaten any chestnuts. She said the Serpent informed her that "chestnut" was a figurative term meaning an aged and mouldy joke.

听了这话，我的脸都变白了，因为我开过许多玩笑来打发无聊的时光，其中有些可能就是她说的那种笑话，虽然我在说那些笑话的时候，确实以为它们是新的。她问我是不是在灾难发生的时候讲了什么笑话。我不得不承认，我当时确实给自己讲了一个，不过没有大声说出来。

I turned pale at that, for I have made many jokes to pass the weary time, and some of them could have been of that sort, though I had honestly supposed that they were new when I made them. She asked me if I had made one just at the time of the catastrophe. I was obliged to admit that I had made one to myself, though not aloud.

情况是这样的，我当时想到了瀑布，我在心里说：“看到这么多水从上面滚落下来，多么美妙啊！”然后刹那间，我脑子里闪过一个聪明的念头，我一时兴起地说道：“要是能看到水从下往上流，那就更妙了！”——这个念头让我笑得不行，就在这时，大自然的一切在战争和死亡中全乱了套，我也只能逃命去了。

It was this. I was thinking about the Falls, and I said to myself, “How wonderful it is to see that vast body of water tumble down there!” Then in an instant a bright thought flashed into my head, and I let it fly, saying, “It would be a deal more wonderful to see it tumble up there!” —and I was just about to kill myself with laughing at it when all nature broke loose in war and death, and I had to flee for my life.

“瞧，”她得意扬扬地说：“这就对了。蛇提到的就是这个笑话，说它是‘第一枚栗子’，还说它与造物主是同时代的。”唉，确实该怪我。真希望我没那么机灵；哎呀，我要是从来没有过那个聪明念头就好了！

“There,” she said, with triumph, “that is just it; the Serpent mentioned that very jest, and called it the First Chestnut, and said it was coeval with the creation.” Alas, I am indeed to blame. Would that I were not witty; oh, would that I had never had that radiant thought!

次年

我们把这个捡来的小家伙叫作“该隐”。我在伊利湖北岸设陷阱捕猎的时候，夏娃抓到了这个小家伙；她在树林里捉到了它，那片树林离我们的地洞几英里远——也许是四英里，她也不确定。

Next Year

We have named it Cain. She caught it while I was up country trapping on the North Shore of the Erie; caught it in the timber a couple of miles from our dug-out—or it might have been four, she isn't certain which.

夏娃觉得它在某些地方与我们很像，可能是我们的亲戚。但我不这么认为。它的体型和我们相差太大，由此可以断定，这是一种不同的新动物——或许是一种鱼，我把它放到水里来看看是不是，它却沉下去了，夏娃跳下水把它抓了回来，实验就此中止，于是也就搞不清了。

It resembles us in some ways, and may be a relation. That is what she thinks, but this is an error, in my judgment. The difference in size warrants the conclusion that it is a different and new kind of animal—a fish, perhaps, though when I put it in the water to see, it sank, and she plunged in and snatched it out before there was opportunity for the experiment to determine the matter.

我还是觉得它是条鱼，但她并不关心它到底是什么，也不让我再拿它去试。我真不明白。这个生物一来，她整个人似乎都变了，对实验很不理智。她经常想着它，对它的关心超过其他所有动物，但又解释不了为什么。

I still think it is a fish, but she is indifferent about what it is, and will not let me have it to try. I do not understand this. The coming of the creature seems to have changed her whole nature and made her unreasonable about experiments. She thinks more of it than she does of any of the other animals, but is not able to explain why.

从很多事上都能看出，她大脑混乱了。有时那条鱼不开心，要到水里去，她就把它抱在怀里，半个晚上都不放下。这时，她脸上用来看东西的地方就会流出水来，她拍着那条鱼的背，嘴里发出轻柔的声音抚慰它，表现出无尽的忧伤和牵挂。我没见过她这样对待其他鱼，这让我很担心。

Her mind is disordered—everything shows it. Sometimes she carries the fish in her arms half the night when it complains and wants to get to the water. At such times the water comes out of the places in her face that she looks out of, and she pats the fish on the back and makes soft sounds with her mouth to soothe it, and betrays sorrow and solicitude in a hundred ways. I have never seen her do like this with any other fish, and it troubles me greatly.

以前，在我们没有失去伊甸园的时候，她也曾这样抱小老虎，与它们玩耍，但也只是与它们玩儿；如果老虎不喜欢它们的晚餐，她也不会像现在这样激动。

She used to carry the young tigers around so, and play with them, before we lost our property; but it was only play; she never took on about them like this when their dinner disagreed with them.

星期天

她在星期天不干活，就躺在那儿，看起来疲惫不堪。她喜欢让那条鱼在她身上打滚，还发出傻傻的声音逗它开心，假装要咬它的爪子，这会让它大笑起来。以前我从未见过会笑的鱼。这让我很想不通……我开始喜欢上星期天了。整整一星期的工作让身体累得够呛。星期天应该更多一些。我以前觉得星期天很难熬，但现在，有星期天可真不错。

Sunday

She doesn't work Sundays, but lies around all tired out, and likes to have the fish wallow over her; and she makes fool noises to amuse it, and pretends to chew its paws, and that makes it laugh. I have not seen a fish before that could laugh. This makes me doubt.... I have come to like Sunday myself. Superintending all the week tires a body so. There ought to be more Sundays. In the old days they were tough, but now they come in handy.

星期三

它不是鱼。究竟是什么我也不太清楚。它如果感到不满，就会发出奇怪的、魔鬼似的声音；感到满足的时候就会“咕咕”叫。我觉得它跟我们不是同类，因为它不走路；也不是鸟，因为它不会飞；也不是青蛙，因为它不会跳；也不是蛇，因为它不爬行。虽然我无法知道它究竟会不会游泳，但我确定它不是鱼。

Wednesday

It isn't a fish. I cannot quite make out what it is. It makes curious, devilish noises when not satisfied, and says "goo-goo" when it is. It is not one of us, for it doesn't walk; it is not a bird, for it doesn't fly; it is not a frog, for it doesn't hop; it is not a snake, for it doesn't crawl; I feel sure it is not a fish, though I cannot get a chance to find out whether it can swim or not.

它常常脸朝上，四脚朝天地躺着。我从没见过其他动物这样做。我说它是个谜；可她只是钦佩“谜”这个字眼，并不理解真正的意思。在我看来，它要么是个谜，要么就是种虫子。如果它死了，我就把它打开，看看它的构造。从来没什么东西让我如此困惑。

It merely lies around, and mostly on its back, with its feet up. I have not seen any other animal do that before. I said I believed it was an enigma, but she only admired the word without understanding it. In my judgment it is either an enigma or some kind of a bug. If it dies, I will take it apart and see what its arrangements are. I never had a thing perplex me so.

三个月后

我的困惑没有减少，反而增加了。我睡得很少。它现在已经不愿意躺着，而是开始用四条腿到处爬行。可是它的前腿特别短，和其他四条腿的动物都不一样。结果，它身体的大部分都别扭地立在空中，这可真不好看。

Three Months Later

The perplexity augments instead of diminishing. I sleep but little. It has ceased from lying around, and goes about on its four legs now. Yet it differs from the other four-legged animals in that its front legs are unusually short, consequently this causes the main part of its person to stick up uncomfortably high in the air, and this is not attractive.

它的身体和我们差不多，但它走路的样子说明它和我们不是同类。它前肢短、后肢长，这说明它属于袋鼠科，但它显然是个变种，因为真正的袋鼠会跳，它却不跳。不过，它是一种奇特而有趣的变种，此前都没有相关记载。

It is built much as we are, but its method of travelling shows that it is not of our breed. The short front legs and long hind ones indicate that it is of the kangaroo family, but it is a marked variation of the species, since the true kangaroo hops, whereas this one never does. Still, it is a curious and interesting variety, and has not been catalogued before.

既然这一点是由我发现的，我觉得应该让它冠上我的名字，来显示这份荣耀，于是我称之为亚当袋鼠……

As I discovered it, I have felt justified in securing the credit of the discovery by attaching my name to it, and hence have called it Kangaroorum Adamiensis....

它来的时候，应该还是个幼崽，因为它后来一直在长。它现在肯定有刚来时五倍那么大，不满足时发出的声音也更大，是一开始的二十二到三十八倍。威吓没法让它安静，还会适得其反。于是我放弃了这个办法。夏娃则轻声安抚来让它安静，或者给它点东西，她之前明明跟我说不会给它。

It must have been a young one when it came, for it has grown exceedingly since. It must be five times as big, now, as it was then, and when discontented is able to make from twenty-two to thirty-eight times the noise it made at first. Coercion does not modify this, but has the contrary effect. For this reason I discontinued the system. She reconciles it by persuasion, and by giving it things which she had previously told it she wouldn't give it.

前面说过，当初它来的时候，我不在家，夏娃对我说，她是在树林里找到这个小东西的。如果说它独自一个、没有同类，似乎有些奇怪，但实际情况好像真是这样，因为最近几个星期，我疲于再找一个这样的生物来扩充收藏，还能跟它做个玩伴——如果有个伴儿，它肯定要安静一点吧，这样我们就能更轻易地驯服它。但我一个都没找到，也没有发现它的同类留下的痕迹，而最奇怪的是，没有脚印。

As already observed, I was not at home when it first came, and she told me she found it in the woods. It seems odd that it should be the only one, yet it must be so, for I have worn myself out these many weeks trying to find another one to add to my collection, and for this one to play with; for surely then it would be quieter, and we could tame it more easily. But I find none, nor any vestige of any; and strangest of all, no tracks.

它肯定生活在陆地上，这一点毋庸置疑；那么，它怎么能四处走动而不留下脚印呢？我设了十多个陷阱，抓到了所有小动物，也没抓到像它这样的小东西。我想，那些动物完全是出于好奇才走进陷阱，它们就是想看看放在那儿的奶是干吗用的。它们并不喝奶。

It has to live on the ground, it cannot help itself; therefore, how does it get about without leaving a track? I have set a dozen traps, but they do no good. I catch all small animals except that one; animals that merely go into the trap out of curiosity, I think, to see what the milk is there for. They never drink it.

又三个月后

这只袋鼠还在长，真是奇怪，让人疑惑。我从没见过别的袋鼠要花这么久的时间长大。现在它脑袋上长出了毛，不像袋鼠的毛，倒和我们的头发一模一样，不过更细、更软，不是黑色而是红色的。

Three Months Later

The kangaroo still continues to grow, which is very strange and perplexing. I never knew one to be so long getting its growth. It has fur on its head now; not like kangaroo fur, but exactly like our hair, except that it is much finer and softer, and instead of being black is red.

这只小怪物在动物学上没法归类，它的生长过程变化莫测、令人烦躁，都要把我逼疯了。要是能再抓到一只就好了——但这不太可能。毫无疑问，这是一种新物种，而且仅此一只。

I am like to lose my mind over the capricious and harassing developments of this unclassifiable zoological freak. If I could catch another one—but that is hopeless; it is a new variety, and the only sample; this is plain.

我觉得它很孤单，一个亲戚也没有，应该会愿意去找只袋鼠做伴，甚至愿意找任何动物，只要对方能让它感到亲近或者给予它同情，毕竟它现在处境凄凉，周围都是不懂它的生活方式和习惯的陌生人，也不懂该怎么做才能让它感到友好，于是我抓了一只真正的袋鼠带回家。但是，我想错了——它一看到袋鼠就发起狂来，于是我相信它以前并没有见过袋鼠。

But I caught a true kangaroo and brought it in, thinking that this one, being lonesome, would rather have that for company than have no kin at all, or any animal it could feel a nearness to or get sympathy from in its forlorn condition here among strangers who do not know its ways or habits, or what to do to make it feel that it is among friends; but it was a mistake—it went into such fits at the sight of the kangaroo that I was convinced it had never seen one before.

这可怜的小动物叫嚷不休，我很怜悯它，却没办法让它开心。我要是能驯服它就好了……但这不可能；我越是努力，结果似乎越糟糕。

I pity the poor noisy little animal, but there is nothing I can do to make it happy. If I could tame it—but that is out of the question; the more I try, the worse I seem to make it.

看着这小东西一阵阵的悲伤和激动，我心里很难过。我想把它放了，可夏娃不答应。这似乎太残忍了，不像她的行事风格，不过她或许是对的。如果放它走，它也许会更孤独，既然我都不能给它找到同伴，它自己怎么能找到呢？

It grieves me to the heart to see it in its little storms of sorrow and passion. I wanted to let it go, but she wouldn't hear of it. That seemed cruel and not like her; and yet she may be right. It might be lonelier than ever; for since I cannot find another one, how could it?

五个月后

它不是袋鼠。肯定不是，因为它能握着夏娃的手指站稳，接着用后肢走几步，然后倒下来。它很可能是某种熊，但又没有尾巴——目前还没有，而且它只有脑袋上长了毛。它还在不断发育——这就有些奇怪了，因为熊的发育比这早很多。

Five Months Later

It is not a kangaroo. No, for it supports itself by holding to her finger, and thus goes a few steps on its hind legs, and then falls down. It is probably some kind of a bear; and yet it has no tail—as yet—and no fur, except on its head. It still keeps on growing—that is a curious circumstance, for bears get their growth earlier than this.

自从灾难降临到我们身上，熊是很危险的，所以，如果这头熊嘴上不戴罩子，在我们住的地方晃来晃去，我会很不放心。我跟她说，如果她愿意把它放了，我就给她抓一只袋鼠，但我的提议没用。我想，她是铁了心要让我们去进行愚蠢的冒险。她脑子出了问题，她以前可不是这个样子。

Bears are dangerous—since our catastrophe—and I shall not be satisfied to have this one prowling about the place much longer without a muzzle on. I have offered to get her a kangaroo if she would let this one go, but it did no good—she is determined to run us into all sorts of foolish risks, I think. She was not like this before she lost her mind.

两个星期后

我查看了它的嘴巴。它只有一颗牙，目前还不算危险。它的尾巴也还没长出来。现在，它比以前更吵闹了——大多是在夜里吵。我已经搬出去了。不过我还是会过去，早上我去吃早饭，顺便看看它有没有长出新牙。等它长出满嘴的牙齿，就该让它离开了，不管它到时有没有尾巴，因为熊就算没有尾巴，也是很危险的。

A Fortnight Later

I examined its mouth. There is no danger yet; it has only one tooth. It has no tail yet. It makes more noise now than it ever did before—and mainly at night. I have moved out. But I shall go over, mornings, to breakfast, and to see if it has more teeth. If it gets a mouthful of teeth, it will be time for it to go, tail or no tail, for a bear does not need a tail in order to be dangerous.

四个月后

我已经在外打猎捕鱼一个月了，就在夏娃取名为“水牛”的地方，我不明白她为什么取这个名字，难道是因为那里根本没有水牛。与此同时，这头熊已经学会了自己用后肢摇摇晃晃地走路，还会说“爸爸”和“妈妈”。

Four Months Later

I have been off hunting and fishing a month, up in the region that she calls Buffalo; I don't know why, unless it is because there are not any buffaloes there. Meantime the bear has learned to paddle around all by itself on its hind legs, and says “poppa” and “momma”.

它肯定是个新物种。它发出的声音很像单词，肯定只是凑巧，并没有什么目的或意义。不过，尽管如此，这也很不寻常了，因为别的熊可都不会。它能模仿人说话，身上基本上没有皮毛，没有尾巴，这充分表明，它是一种新的熊。

It is certainly a new species. This resemblance to words may be purely accidental, of course, and may have no purpose or meaning; but even in that case it is still extraordinary, and is a thing which no other bear can do. This imitation of speech, taken together with general absence of fur and entire absence of tail, sufficiently indicates that this is a new kind of bear.

进一步探究的话，肯定会非常有趣。与此同时，我打算去北方的树林远行，彻底地搜索一番。肯定还有这样的熊在某个地方，如果有同类做伴，这头熊就不那么危险。我马上就动身，但我要先把这头熊的嘴给套住。

The further study of it will be exceedingly interesting. Meantime I will go off on a far expedition among the forests of the North and make an exhaustive search. There must certainly be another one somewhere, and this one will be less dangerous when it has company of its own species. I will go straightway; but I will muzzle this one first.

三个月后

这次搜索很累、很累，而且我一无所获。然而与此同时，夏娃待在家里，竟然又抓了一个它的同类！我从没有这么好的运气。就算我在树林里找个一百年，也遇不到这样的东西。

Three Months Later

It has been a weary, weary hunt, yet I have had no success. In the meantime, without stirring from the home estate, she has caught another one! I never saw such luck. I might have hunted these woods a hundred years, I never should have run across that thing.

次日

我一直在比较新抓住的这只和原来那只，它们显然属于同一物种。我本来想把其中一只做成标本，收藏起来，但不知道为什么，她却反对这种做法，于是我放弃了这个念头，虽然我觉得放弃是个错误。万一它们逃走了，那将是科学上无法弥补的损失。

Next Day

I have been comparing the new one with the old one, and it is perfectly plain that they are the same breed. I was going to stuff one of them for my collection, but she is prejudiced against it for some reason or other; so I have relinquished the idea, though I think it is a mistake. It would be an irreparable loss to science if they should get away.

原来那只比以前更温驯了，它会笑，还会像鹦鹉一样说话。毫无疑问，这是因为它经常和鹦鹉待在一起，而且模仿能力很强。如果它是一种新的鹦鹉，我会感到惊讶；但是，我不该感到惊讶，因为最初那些日子里，它是一条鱼，从那以后，所有能想到的东西，它几乎全都当过。

The old one is tamer than it was, and can laugh and talk like the parrot, having learned this, no doubt, from being with the parrot so much, and having the imitative faculty in a highly developed degree. I shall be astonished if it turns out to be a new kind of parrot, and yet I ought not to be astonished, for it has already been everything else it could think of, since those first days when it was a fish.

新来的很丑，和第一只最初的时候一样；它们都有生肉一般的硫黄色皮肤，都有没毛发的奇特脑袋。夏娃叫它“亚伯”。

The new one is as ugly now as the old one was at first; has the same sulphur-and-raw-meat complexion and the same singular head without any fur on it. She calls it Abel.

十年后

他们其实是男孩；这一点我们很久以前就发现了。只不过他们刚来的时候形态幼小，我们才困惑了很久；那时候我们还不习惯。现在我们还有了几个女孩。亚伯是个好孩子，但如果该隐是头熊，那反而更好。

Ten Years Later

They are boys; we found it out long ago. It was their coming in that small, immature shape that puzzled us; we were not used to it. There are some girls now. Abel is a good boy, but if Cain had stayed a bear it would have improved him.

过了这么多年，我才明白当初对夏娃的看法是错的；一个人住在伊甸园里，不如和她一起住在伊甸园外。起初我觉得她话太多；但现在，如果我的生活中没了她的声音，我会感到难过。愿那枚栗子得到保佑，是它让我们走到一起，让我懂得她心地的善良、精神的甜美！

After all these years, I see that I was mistaken about Eve in the beginning; it is better to live outside the Garden with her than inside it without her. At first I thought she talked too much; but now I should be sorry to have that voice fall silent and pass out of my life. Blessed be the chestnut that brought us near together and taught me to know the goodness of her heart and the sweetness of her spirit!

夏娃日记

星期六

现在，我的年龄差不多是一整天。我是昨天到的。在我看来是这样。大概就是一天吧，如果昨天之前还有时间，我也不在场，不然我应该记得的。当然，也许之前真的有过时间，那我肯定没好好注意之前发生了什么。不过从现在开始我会好好留意，如果还有什么昨天之类的日子到来，我会把它记下来的。

Saturday

I am almost a whole day old, now. I arrived yesterday. That is as it seems to me. And it must be so, for if there was a day-before-yesterday I was not there when it happened, or I should remember it. It could be, of course, that it did happen, and that I was not noticing. Very well; I will be very watchful now, and if any day-before-yesterdays happen I will make a note of it.

最好有个好开头，别记乱了。某种本能告诉我，有朝一日这些记录对于历史研究者会很重要。因为我觉得自己是一个实验品，我感觉就是个实验品，不会有人感觉比我更像，所以我慢慢开始相信，这就是我——实验品；只是个实验品而已。

It will be best to start right and not let the record get confused, for some instinct tells me that these details are going to be important to the historian some day. For I feel like an experiment, I feel exactly like an experiment; it would be impossible for a person to feel more like an experiment than I do, and so I am coming to feel convinced that that is what I AM—an experiment; just an experiment, and nothing more.

如果我是一个实验品，我就是实验的全部吗？不，我想我不是全部，我应该是实验的主要部分，当然还有其他部分，而且其他部分也有各自的责任和作用。

Then if I am an experiment, am I the whole of it? No, I think not; I think the rest of it is part of it. I am the main part of it, but I think the rest of it has its share in the matter.

那么我的地位牢固吗？或者我得小心行事，想办法保住位置？可能是后者吧。某种本能告诉我，高人一等的代价就是要一直警惕。（我想，对于我这么一个年轻的生命来说，这是一句良言。）

Is my position assured, or do I have to watch it and take care of it? The latter, perhaps. Some instinct tells me that eternal vigilance is the price of supremacy. (That is a good phrase, I think, for one so young.)

今天的一切看起来都比昨天更好。昨天太急着完成工作，结果山上一片狼藉，平原上也全是垃圾和残余的材料，各方面都很令人糟心。高贵、美丽的艺术品不应仓促地造就，而这个宏伟的新世界正是一件最为高贵、最美丽的作品。尽管创造它的时间很短，可它近乎完美。

Everything looks better today than it did yesterday. In the rush of finishing up yesterday, the mountains were left in a ragged condition, and some of the plains were so cluttered with rubbish and remnants that the aspects were quite distressing. Noble and beautiful works of art should not be subjected to haste; and this majestic new world is indeed a most noble and beautiful work. And certainly marvelously near to being perfect, notwithstanding the shortness of the time.

虽然有些地方的星星太多，有些地方的星星又不够，但毫无疑问，这些都能很快补救。昨晚，月亮变得松动，从天边滑了下去，跌出了这伟大的宏图——真是个大损失。一想到这我就心碎。在所有的装饰物中，没有什么能比得上它的华丽和完美。我们本就应该把它固定得更牢一些。要是我们能把月亮弄回来就好了……

There are too many stars in some places and not enough in others, but that can be remedied presently, no doubt. The moon got loose last night, and slid down and fell out of the scheme—a very great loss; it breaks my heart to think of it. There isn't another thing among the ornaments and decorations that is comparable to it for beauty and finish. It should have been fastened better. If we can only get it back again—

当然，谁也不知道月亮去了哪里。而且，无论谁得到它，都会藏起来。我知道，因为我自己就会这样做。我相信在其他事情上我都会诚实，但我已经意识到，在我的天性里，在我灵魂的深处充满对美的热爱与渴求。我还意识到，如果月亮属于别人，那个人又不知道月亮在我手上，那么把月亮交给我是不安全的。

But of course there is no telling where it went to. And besides, whoever gets it will hide it; I know it because I would do it myself. I believe I can be honest in all other matters, but I already begin to realize that the core and center of my nature is love of the beautiful, a passion for the beautiful, and that it would not be safe to trust me with a moon that belonged to another person and that person didn't know I had it.

如果我在白天找到了月亮，我可以放弃，因为我会害怕有人也在看着它；但如果我在黑暗中找到了月亮，我肯定会找到某种借口，不透露任何消息。因为我真的爱月亮，它那么美丽，那么浪漫。我真希望有五六个月亮，这样我就永远不睡觉，而是一直躺在长着苔藓的河岸上，永不觉疲倦地仰望它们。

I could give up a moon that I found in the daytime, because I should be afraid someone was looking; but if I found it in the dark, I am sure I should find some kind of an excuse for not saying anything about it. For I do love moons, they are so pretty and so romantic. I wish we had five or six; I would never go to bed; I should never get tired lying on the moss-bank and looking up at them.

星星也很美丽。我想抓一些下来，放到头发上。但我想，我永远也做不到。虽然它们看上去很近，却与我相距甚远。昨天晚上，星星刚亮起来的时候，我试着拿一根杆子想打一些下来，但根本够不到，这让我吃了一惊；然后我又试着用土块砸，直到累得筋疲力尽，我也没能打到一颗。因为我是左撇子，扔得又不准。

Stars are good, too. I wish I could get some to put in my hair. But I suppose I never can. You would be surprised to find how far off they are, for they do not look it. When they first showed, last night, I tried to knock some down with a pole, but it didn't reach, which astonished me; then I tried clods till I was all tired out, but I never got one. It was because I am left-handed and cannot throw good.

即使我朝着想要的星星旁边瞄准，还是打不中旁边的某一颗。不过有几次差点就成功了，因为我看见土块像个黑点一样，直直射入金黄色的星群中间，有四五十次吧，只差一点就能打中了，如果我再多坚持一会儿，或许就能打下一颗星星了。

Even when I aimed at the one I wasn't after I couldn't hit the other one, though I did make some close shots, for I saw the black blot of the clod sail right into the midst of the golden clusters forty or fifty times, just barely missing them, and if I could have held out a little longer maybe I could have got one.

于是我哭了一会儿，我想以我现在的年龄，会哭也是很自然的吧。休息了一会儿后，我拿起一只篮子，朝最边缘的地方走去，那儿的星星离地面很近，我用手就能摘到，这样更好，因为我可以温柔地摘，不会把星星摔下来弄坏。但是那地方比我想象中要远得多，最后我只好放弃。我筋疲力尽，连半步都迈不动了，而且两只脚都疼得要命。

So I cried a little, which was natural, I suppose, for one of my age, and after I was rested I got a basket and started for a place on the extreme rim of the circle, where the stars were close to the ground and I could get them with my hands, which would be better, anyway, because I could gather them tenderly then, and not break them. But it was farther than I thought, and at last I had to give it up. I was so tired I couldn't drag my feet another step; and besides, they were sore and hurt me very much.

我没法回家了。路太远，天气也渐渐冷了下来，不过我遇到了几只老虎，我依偎在它们中间，真是又暖和又舒服。老虎以草莓为生，呼吸中都带着甜味。我虽然从没见过老虎，但看到它们的斑纹我就认出来了。如果能有一张那样的毛皮，我会做一件漂亮的大衣。

I couldn't get back home; it was too far and turning cold; but I found some tigers and nestled in among them and was most adorably comfortable, and their breath was sweet and pleasant, because they live on strawberries. I had never seen a tiger before, but I knew them in a minute by the stripes. If I could have one of those skins, it would make a lovely gown.

今天，我对距离有了更好的认识。我总是很心急，遇上令我眼花缭乱的漂亮事物，我就会很冒失地去抓。有时它离我太远，抓不到；有时它离我有六英寸，但看起来是一英尺——唉，那是因为中间还有荆棘！于是我得到了人生的第一次教训，还编了一句格言，是我自己想出来的：**实验品被划到，遇到荆棘要躲开**。我觉得这句格言编得特别好，毕竟我年龄很小。

Today I am getting better ideas about distances. I was so eager to get hold of every pretty thing that I giddily grabbed for it, sometimes when it was too far off, and sometimes when it was but six inches away but seemed a foot—alas, with thorns between! I learned a lesson; also I made an axiom, all out of my own head—my very first one; THE SCRATCHED EXPERIMENT SHUNS THE THORN. I think it is a very good one for one so young.

昨天下午，我隔着一段距离跟在另一个实验品后面，想看看它是用来做什么的。但我没能弄清楚。我想它应该是个男人。我从来没有见过男人，但它看起来像，我确信它就是。我意识到，我对它的好奇心比对其他任何爬行动物都要强。

I followed the other Experiment around, yesterday afternoon, at a distance, to see what it might be for, if I could. But I was not able to make [it] out. I think it is a man. I had never seen a man, but it looked like one, and I feel sure that that is what it is. I realize that I feel more curiosity about it than about any of the other reptiles.

它是不是一只爬行动物呢，我觉得它是。因为它有蓬乱的头发，蓝色的眼睛，所以看起来像爬行动物。它没有臀部，身体像胡萝卜一样从上到下渐渐变细；它站立时会全身展开，像井架一样；所以我觉得它是爬行动物，不过它也可能只是个搭建起来的事物。

If it is a reptile, and I suppose it is; for it has frowzy hair and blue eyes, and looks like a reptile. It has no hips; it tapers like a carrot; when it stands, it spreads itself apart like a derrick; so I think it is a reptile, though it may be architecture.

一开始我很害怕，每次它一转身我就开始跑，因为我以为它是要追我；但是，我渐渐发现它只是想把我甩开，从那以后我就不害怕了，而是跟在它后面大约二十码的地方，跟了它好几个小时，这让它很紧张，很不高兴。最后它很担心，竟然爬到一棵树上。我等了好一会儿，最后放弃了，回了家。

I was afraid of it at first, and started to run every time it turned around, for I thought it was going to chase me; but by and by I found it was only trying to get away, so after that I was not timid any more, but tracked it along, several hours, about twenty yards behind, which made it nervous and unhappy. At last it was a good deal worried, and climbed a tree. I waited a good while, then gave it up and went home.

今天也发生了同样的事。我又一次把它追到树上去了。

Today the same thing over. I've got it up the tree again.

星期天

它还在树上，看上去是在休息。但那只是做样子罢了：星期天可不是休息的日子；星期六才是指定的休息日。在我看来，它好像只对休息感兴趣。如果让我一直这么歇着，我会累得不行。在树旁边坐着看，我都觉得累。我真不明白它有什么用处；我从没见它做过什么事。

Sunday

It is up there yet. Resting, apparently. But that is a subterfuge: Sunday isn't the day of rest; Saturday is appointed for that. It looks to me like a creature that is more interested in resting than in anything else. It would tire me to rest so much. It tires me just to sit around and watch the tree. I do wonder what it is for; I never see it do anything.

昨天晚上，他们把月亮还了回来，我特别高兴。我觉得他们这样做非常诚实。虽然月亮后来又掉了下去，但有这样的邻居，就没有必要担心；他们会把月亮找回来的。我真希望能做点什么来表达感激。我想送给他们一些星星，因为我们有太多用不上的星星了。不对，是我，不是我们，因为我知道那只爬行动物对这种事根本不关心。

They returned the moon last night, and I was SO happy! I think it is very honest of them. It slid down and fell off again, but I was not distressed; there is no need to worry when one has that kind of neighbors; they will fetch it back. I wish I could do something to show my appreciation. I would like to send them some stars, for we have more than we can use. I mean I, not we, for I can see that the reptile cares nothing for such things.

它口味很差，也不善良。昨天傍晚，当我到那儿去的时候，它已经爬了下来，在抓池塘里玩耍的带斑点的小鱼，我只好拿土块打它，它这才放过小鱼，又爬到树上去。我很疑惑，难道这就是它的作用？它是铁石心肠吗？难道它对这些小动物没有一点同情心？会不会它被设计出来就是为了做这种狠心的事情呢？看样子，它的确像。

It has low tastes, and is not kind. When I went there yesterday evening in the gloaming it had crept down and was trying to catch the little speckled fishes that play in the pool, and I had to clod it to make it go up the tree again and let them alone. I wonder if THAT is what it is for? Hasn't it any heart? Hasn't it any compassion for those little creature? Can it be that it was designed and manufactured for such ungentle work? It has the look of it.

有一块土块砸在它耳后，它竟然开口说话了。我感到很惊讶，这是我第一次听到除我之外的人说话。它说的词语我不明白，不过似乎很有表现力。

One of the clods took it back of the ear, and it used language. It gave me a thrill, for it was the first time I had ever heard speech, except my own. I did not understand the words, but they seemed expressive.

发现它会说话之后，我对它有了新的兴趣，因为我喜欢说话，我整天都在说话，睡觉的时候也说，而且我也很有趣；但是，如果有另一个人可以和我说话，我就能比现在有趣一倍，只要对方愿意，我可以一直说下去。

When I found it could talk I felt a new interest in it, for I love to talk; I talk, all day, and in my sleep, too, and I am very interesting, but if I had another to talk to I could be twice as interesting, and would never stop, if desired.

如果这只爬行动物是个男人，那它就不应该叫“它”，不是吗？那样不符合语法。我觉得应该用“他”。我觉得是这样。那么，语法上就该这么用：主格，He；宾格，Him；形容词，His'n[1]。好了，我以后就把它当作男人，先称它为“他”，除非它又变成其他东西。这样会更方便些，没那么多不确定性。

If this reptile is a man, it isn't an IT, is it? That wouldn't be grammatical, would it? I think it would be HE. I think so. In that case one would parse it thus: nominative, HE; dative, HIM; possessive, HIS'N. Well, I will consider it a man and call it he until it turns out to be something else. This will be handier than having so many uncertainties.

① his'n 是 his 的非标准形式，方言。

下星期天

整整一个星期，我一直跟在他身后，想跟他熟悉起来。我必须主动和他交流，因为他很害羞，不过我不介意。有我在身边，他似乎很高兴，我试着在对话中用“我们”这个交际用词，把他也包括在内，他对这一点似乎很满意。

Next Week Sunday

All the week I tagged around after him and tried to get acquainted. I had to do the talking, because he was shy, but I didn't mind it. He seemed pleased to have me around, and I used the sociable "we" a good deal, because it seemed to flatter him to be included.

星期三

现在，我们相处得真的很好，也越来越熟悉了。他不再想办法躲着我，这是个好现象，说明他喜欢我在身边。这让我很高兴，我也尽量试着去帮助他，让他更重视我。

Wednesday

We are getting along very well indeed, now, and getting better and better acquainted. He does not try to avoid me any more, which is a good sign, and shows that he likes to have me with him. That pleases me, and I study to be useful to him in every way I can, so as to increase his regard.

最近这一两天，我把命名的工作从他手里全接下来了，这让他大大地松了口气，因为他在取名上没有一点天赋，显然他也很感激我能替他完成工作。他取不出合理的名字来挽回面子，我看出了他的不足，但没让他知道。

During the last day or two I have taken all the work of naming things off his hands, and this has been a great relief to him, for he has no gift in that line, and is evidently very grateful. He can't think of a rational name to save him, but I do not let him see that I am aware of his defect.

每当一个新生物出现，我就马上说出名字，不然一阵令人难堪的沉默后，他就会显露他的不足。通过这种方式我多次让他免于尴尬。只要看到某个动物，我立刻就知道那是什么。我不需要思考，正确的名字马上就会从我脑海中自动跳出来，就像是灵光一闪，毫无疑问就是灵光一闪，因为我半分钟前还不知道那名字呢。好像我根据动物的外形和行动的方式，就能知道那是什么。

Whenever a new creature comes along I name it before he has time to expose himself by an awkward silence. In this way I have saved him many embarrassments. I have no defect like this. The minute I set eyes on an animal I know what it is. I don't have to reflect a moment; the right name comes out instantly, just as if it were an inspiration, as no doubt it is, for I am sure it wasn't in me half a minute before. I seem to know just by the shape of the creature and the way it acts what animal it is.

遇到渡渡鸟的时候，我能从他眼睛里看出来，他以为那是野猫。但我挽救了他的颜面，还处理得很小心，以免伤害他的尊严。我就很自然地提高声音，以表示这是个意外之喜，没露出任何想要传达信息的意思，我说："呀，我在此宣布，那不就是渡渡鸟嘛！"

When the dodo came along he thought it was a wildcat—I saw it in his eye. But I saved him. And I was careful not to do it in a way that could hurt his pride. I just spoke up in a quite natural way of pleasing surprise, and not as if I was dreaming of conveying information, and said, "Well, I do declare, if there isn't the dodo!"

我轻描淡写地向他解释我是怎么知道这是渡渡鸟的。这种生物我知道，他却不知道，我觉得他也许为此有点气恼，但是，他显然很佩服我。这让我很开心，睡觉之前，我满足地回想了好几遍。当我们感到有收获时，哪怕是一件很小的事情也会令我们开心！

I explained—without seeming to be explaining—how I know it for a dodo, and although I thought maybe he was a little piqued that I knew the creature when he didn't, it was quite evident that he admired me. That was very agreeable, and I thought of it more than once with gratification before I slept. How little a thing can make us happy when we feel that we have earned it!

星期四

这是我第一次感到伤心。昨天，他躲开了我，似乎希望我以后都不要和他讲话了。我无法相信，以为发生了什么误会，因为我喜欢和他在一起，我喜欢听他说话，那他怎么会对我没有好感呢？我什么也没有做啊。

Thursday

My first sorrow. Yesterday he avoided me and seemed to wish I would not talk to him. I could not believe it, and thought there was some mistake, for I loved to be with him, and loved to hear him talk, and so how could it be that he could feel unkind toward me when I had not done anything?

但最后，情况好像真的是这样，于是我走开了，独自到我初次见到他的地方坐着。那天上午我们被创造出来，当时我还不知道他是谁，对他很冷淡。可是，现在这里成了个悲伤的地方，每处小事物都昭示着他的存在，我心里非常难过。因为这是一种新的情感，我不清楚为什么会这样。以前我没有经历过，这一切都是谜，我无法理解。

But at last it seemed true, so I went away and sat lonely in the place where I first saw him the morning that we were made and I did not know what he was and was indifferent about him; but now it was a mournful place, and every little thing spoke of him, and my heart was very sore. I did not know why very clearly, for it was a new feeling; I had not experienced it before, and it was all a mystery, and I could not make it out.

但当夜幕降临时，我无法忍受这种孤独，便跑到他建造的新房子里，问他我做错了什么，怎样才能弥补过错，重新得到他的善意。可他把我赶到雨里，这是我第一次伤心。

But when night came I could not bear the lonesomeness, and went to the new shelter which he has built, to ask him what I had done that was wrong and how I could mend it and get back his kindness again; but he put me out in the rain, and it was my first sorrow.

星期天

现在又好了，我又开心起来。虽然那些天我很难过；但我可以忍住不去想那些日子。

我想弄一些苹果给他，可我总是扔不直，所以总打不中。虽然我失败了，不过我想我的好意会让他高兴的。可他说那是禁果，如果我采摘的话，会受到伤害。但是，只要让他高兴，即使受到伤害，我为什么要在乎呢？伤害又有什么关系？

Sunday

It is pleasant again, now, and I am happy; but those were heavy days; I do not think of them when I can help it.

I tried to get him some of those apples, but I cannot learn to throw straight. I failed, but I think the good intention pleased him. They are forbidden, and he says I shall come to harm; but so I come to harm through pleasing him, why shall I care for that harm?

星期一

今天上午，我把我的名字告诉了他，希望他会感兴趣。可他并不在乎。这很奇怪。如果他肯把名字告诉我，我会在乎的。我想，他的名字将是我听过的最悦耳的声音。

Monday

This morning I told him my name, hoping it would interest him. But he did not care for it. It is strange. If he should tell me his name, I would care. I think it would be pleasanter in my ears than any other sound.

他很少说话。也许是因为他不聪明，对这一点比较敏感，不希望别人知道。他竟会这样想，真是太可惜了。因为聪明根本算不了什么，一个人的价值在于心灵。真希望我能让他明白，一颗充满爱与善良的心灵才是财富，有这样一颗心，人生才是富足的，若没有，即便拥有智慧，人生也是贫乏的。

He talks very little. Perhaps it is because he is not bright, and is sensitive about it and wishes to conceal it. It is such a pity that he should feel so, for brightness is nothing; it is in the heart that the values lie. I wish I could make him understand that a loving good heart is riches, and riches enough, and that without it intellect is poverty.

他虽然话少，词汇量却相当丰富。今天早上，他用了一个出人意料的好词。显然，他自己也意识到那是个好词，因为后来他又漫不经心地用了两次。他那漫不经心的样子，装得可不好，不过这仍旧说明，他拥有某种可进一步完善的品格。毫无疑问，这就像是种子一样，只要加以照料，就能生根发芽。

Although he talks so little, he has quite a considerable vocabulary. This morning he used a surprisingly good word. He evidently recognized, himself, that it was a good one, for he worked it in twice afterward, casually. It was good casual art, still it showed that he possesses a certain quality of perception. Without a doubt that seed can be made to grow, if cultivated.

他是从哪儿学来的这个词呢？我以前可从来没用过。

他对我的名字不感兴趣。我努力不露出失望的情绪，但我想我藏得并不好。我走开了，坐在长着青苔的岸上，双脚浸在水里。

Where did he get that word? I do not think I have ever used it.

No, he took no interest in my name. I tried to hide my disappointment, but I suppose I did not succeed. I went away and sat on the moss-bank with my feet in the water.

如果我渴望身边有个人陪着，可以看看、说说话，那我就会到这儿来。水中有个可爱的白色身影，虽然不够，但总比彻底的孤独要好。我说话的时候，它也说话；我伤心的时候，它也伤心；它会对我表示同情，以此来安慰我。它说："不要难过，没有朋友的可怜女孩。我来当你的朋友。"它真的成了我的好朋友，也是我唯一的好朋友；它是我的姐妹。

It is where I go when I hunger for companionship, some one to look at, some one to talk to. It is not enough—that lovely white body painted there in the pool—but it is something, and something is better than utter loneliness. It talks when I talk; it is sad when I am sad; it comforts me with its sympathy; it says, "Do not be downhearted, you poor friendless girl; I will be your friend." It IS a good friend to me, and my only one; it is my sister.

那是我的姐妹第一次抛弃我！唉，我永远不会忘记——永远不会。我的心变成了身体里的一个铅块！我说："她曾是我的一切，可现在她走了！"我感到绝望，我说："我的心碎了，我再也活不下去了！"我用双手捂住脸，伤心欲绝、痛失慰藉。等我把手拿开，过了一会儿，她又出现了，又白又美，光彩照人，我立即跳进了她的怀抱！

That first time that she forsook me! ah, I shall never forget that—never, never. My heart was lead in my body! I said, "She was all I had, and now she is gone!" In my despair I said, "Break, my heart; I cannot bear my life any more!" and hid my face in my hands, and there was no solace for me. And when I took them away, after a little, there she was again, white and shining and beautiful, and I sprang into her arms!

这真是完美的幸福。我之前也体会过幸福的滋味，但和这不一样，这是极乐。从那以后，我再也没有怀疑过她。有时候她会不在——也许一个小时，也许差不多整整一天——但我会等着，心中毫不怀疑。我说："她或许很忙，或许是旅行去了，但她一定会回来的。"的确如此，她总会回来。

That was perfect happiness; I had known happiness before, but it was not like this, which was ecstasy. I never doubted her afterward. Sometimes she stayed away—maybe an hour, maybe almost the whole day, but I waited and did not doubt; I said, "She is busy, or she is gone on a journey, but she will come." And it was so: she always did.

晚上，如果天黑，她就不来了，因为她很胆小；如果有月亮，她就会来。我不害怕黑暗，但她出生得比我晚，比我更小。我去她那儿看了她很多次，当我的生活异常艰难时——生活大多如此，她就是我的慰藉、我的避难所。

At night she would not come if it was dark, for she was a timid little thing; but if there was a moon she would come. I am not afraid of the dark, but she is younger than I am; she was born after I was. Many and many are the visits I have paid her; she is my comfort and my refuge when my life is hard—and it is mainly that.

星期二

整个上午我都在干活，改善这个地方；我故意躲着他，希望他会感到孤单，然后来找我。可他并没有来。中午，我停下来休息了一会儿，和蜜蜂、蝴蝶一起玩耍，陶醉在花香中，这些美丽的花朵能捕捉到上帝的微笑，还保存了下来！我采集花朵，做成了花环和花冠，戴着它们吃了午饭——午饭当然是苹果——然后，我坐在树荫下，盼望着、等待着。但他没有来。

Tuesday

All the morning I was at work improving the estate; and I purposely kept away from him in the hope that he would get lonely and come. But he did not. At noon I stopped for the day and took my recreation by flitting all about with the bees and the butterflies and reveling in the flowers, those beautiful creatures that catch the smile of God out of the sky and preserve it! I gathered them, and made them into wreaths and garlands and clothed myself in them while I ate my luncheon—apples, of course; then I sat in the shade and wished and waited. But he did not come.

不过没关系。就算他来了，也不会有什么结果，因为他不喜欢花。他说花是垃圾，也分不清楚不同的花，还因此觉得自己高人一等。

But no matter. Nothing would have come of it, for he does not care for flowers. He called them rubbish, and cannot tell one from another, and thinks it is superior to feel like that.

他不在乎我，不在乎花，不在乎黄昏时如画的天空——他到底在乎什么呢？难道是造些小棚子，把自己关在里面，躲开干净美妙的雨水？然后拍拍瓜、尝尝葡萄、用手指摸摸树上的水果，看看属于他的东西长势如何？

He does not care for me, he does not care for flowers, he does not care for the painted sky at eventide—is there anything he does care for, except building shacks to coop himself up in from the good clean rain, and thumping the melons, and sampling the grapes, and fingering the fruit on the trees, to see how those properties are coming along?

我把一根干树枝放在地上，用另一根树枝在上面钻洞，本来是想实行原有的计划，但很快我就吓到了。一层薄薄的、透明的、略带蓝色的东西，从那个小洞里冒了出来，我扔下所有的东西，撒腿就跑！我以为那是幽灵，我吓坏了！

I laid a dry stick on the ground and tried to bore a hole in it with another one, in order to carry out a scheme that I had, and soon I got an awful fright. A thin, transparent bluish film rose out of the hole, and I dropped everything and ran! I thought it was a spirit, and I WAS so frightened!

请在微信公众号留言回复以下信息，精彩留言可参与定期抽奖活动。

1. 您购买的图书产品书名
2. 您得知该图书产品的渠道
3. 该图书产品吸引或打动您的理由
4. 您对我司或我司产品的建议

但我回头一看，那幽灵并没有跟来；于是我靠在一块石头上休息，四肢抖个不停，等手脚慢慢稳下来，我又小心翼翼地往回走。我全神警惕着，准备一有情况就随时逃开。我走到近前，拨开一丛玫瑰的枝叶，向里面望。我心里期盼那个男人就在附近，因为我看起来既狡黠又漂亮。但那个幽灵已经不见了。

But I looked back, and it was not coming; so I leaned against a rock and rested and panted, and let my limbs go on trembling until they got steady again; then I crept warily back, alert, watching, and ready to fly if there was occasion; and when I was come near, I parted the branches of a rose-bush and peeped through—wishing the man was about, I was looking so cunning and pretty—but the sprite was gone.

我走过去，小洞里面有一撮细细的粉色灰尘。我用一根手指去摸，“哎哟”一声叫了出来，立即又把手指拿了出来。真是痛死了。我把指头放进嘴里，先用一只脚站着，然后又换另一只脚，嘴里哼个不停，我用这个办法缓解了疼痛。然后我开始仔细查看，心里十分好奇。

I went there, and there was a pinch of delicate pink dust in the hole. I put my finger in, to feel it, and said OUCH! and took it out again. It was a cruel pain. I put my finger in my mouth; and by standing first on one foot and then the other, and grunting, I presently eased my misery; then I was full of interest, and began to examine.

我很想知道那粉色的灰尘是什么。突然，我想到了它的名字，虽然我以前从没听说过。这是火！这一点我绝对肯定。所以我毫不犹豫地给它取了名字——火。

I was curious to know what the pink dust was. Suddenly the name of it occurred to me, though I had never heard of it before. It was FIRE! I was as certain of it as a person could be of anything in the world. So without hesitation I named it that—fire.

我创造了一种以前并不存在的事物；我为这多彩的世界增添了一份新财富。我意识到了这一点，为自己的成就感到自豪，我打算跑去找他，把这件事告诉他，让他更加尊重我——但我考虑了一下，没有这样做。不，他不会在乎的。他会问这有什么用，那我怎么回答呢？因为它除了美并没有什么用处，只是美而已……

I had created something that didn't exist before; I had added a new thing to the world's uncountable properties; I realized this, and was proud of my achievement, and was going to run and find him and tell him about it, thinking to raise myself in his esteem—but I reflected, and did not do it. No—he would not care for it. He would ask what it was good for, and what could I answer? for if it was not *good* for something, but only beautiful, merely beautiful—

于是我叹了口气，没有去。因为它没什么用处；它不能造棚子、不能改良西瓜、不能让水果熟得更快。它没有用，就是个愚蠢、虚荣的东西。他会鄙视，说一些尖刻的话。

So I sighed, and did not go. For it wasn't good for anything; it could not build a shack, it could not imprcve melons, it could not hurry a fruit crop; it was useless, it was a foolishness and a vanity; he would despise it and say cutting words.

但我不会鄙视它；我会说："啊，你这火啊，我爱你，你这精致的、粉红色的小东西，只因你十分美丽——这就够了！"我有一种想把它抱在胸前的欲望。但我忍住了。接着，我大脑里又想到了一条格言，不过这一条和遇到荆棘时那条很像，恐怕只能算是抄袭："**被烫到过，就会躲开火焰**。"

But to me it was not despicable; I said, "Oh, you fire, I love you, you dainty pink creature, for you are BEAUTIFUL—and that is enough!" and was going to gather it to my breast. But refrained. Then I made another maxim out of my head, though it was so nearly like the first one that I was afraid it was only a plagiarism:

THE BURNT EXPERIMENT SHUNS THE FIRE.

我又开始干活：我先做了很多火尘，然后倒在一把褐色的干草上，打算把它带回家，一直留着，和它一起玩，但是风吹到了它，它一下蹿起来，恶狠狠地冲我扑过来，我丢下它就跑。等我回头看的时候，那蓝色的精灵已经长得又高又大，然后身体展开，像云一般翻滚而去，我立刻想到了它的名字——烟！——但我发誓，我从没听说过“烟”这个词。

I wrought again; and when I had made a good deal of fire-dust I emptied it into a handful of dry brown grass, intending to carry it home and keep it always and play with it; but the wind struck it and it sprayed up and spat out at me fiercely, and I dropped it and ran. When I looked back the blue spirit was towering up and stretching and rolling away like a cloud, and instantly I thought of the name of it—SMOKE!—though,upon my word, I had never heard of smoke before.

很快，黄色和红色的明亮火焰在烟雾中蹿起，我不假思索地叫出它的名字——火焰——我取的名字是对的，虽然这是世界上第一次出现火焰。火焰爬到树上，烟雾越来越多，然后火焰在翻滚的烟雾中闪动着耀眼的光。我欣喜若狂，不自觉地拍起手来，又唱又跳，这真是又新奇又美妙！

Soon brilliant yellow and red flares shot up through the smoke, and I named them in an instant—FLAMES—and I was right, too, though these were the very first flames that had ever been in the world. They climbed the trees, then flashed splendidly in and out of the vast and increasing volume of tumbling smoke, and I had to clap my hands and laugh and dance in my rapture, it was so new and strange and so wonderful and so beautiful!

他跑过来，停下脚步盯着看，好久也没说一句话。然后他问那是什么。啊，他竟然问了这么直接的问题，真糟糕。当然，我必须回答，我也回答了。我说这是火。我知道它是什么，而他却不得不来问我。如果他因此生气，那也不是我的错，我并不想惹他生气。他停了一会儿，问道："它是怎么来的？"

He came running, and stopped and gazed, and said not a word for many minutes. Then he asked what it was. Ah, it was too bad that he should ask such a direct question. I had to answer it, of course, and I did. I said it was fire. If it annoyed him that I should know and he must ask; that was not my fault; I had no desire to annoy him. After a pause he asked: "How did it come?"

又一个直接的问题，同样也必须有一个直接的答案："我造出来的。"

火焰越烧越远。他来到被火烧过的地方的边缘，站在那儿低头看着，然后说："这些都是什么？"

"炭。"

他捡起一块想仔细看看，但随即改变了主意，又放下了。然后他走了。他对什么都不感兴趣。

Another direct question, and it also had to have a direct answer.

"I made it."

The fire was traveling farther and farther off. He went to the edge of the burned place and stood looking down, and said:

"What are these?"

"Fire-coals."

He picked up one to examine it, but changed his mind and put it down again. Then he went away. NOTHING interests him.

但是，我很感兴趣。那是灰烬，灰色的，柔软纤细，很漂亮——我立刻就知道了它的名字。还有，余烬；余烬我也知道。我找到了我的苹果，把它们扒了出来，我很高兴自己很年轻、胃口很好。但是，苹果都烤得裂开坏掉了，这让我很失望。表面看来是不能吃了，但其实不是——这比生的更好吃。火是美丽的；我想，总有一天它也会有用。

But I was interested. There were ashes, gray and soft and delicate and pretty—I knew what they were at once. And the embers; I knew the embers, too. I found my apples, and raked them out, and was glad; for I am very young and my appetite is active. But I was disappointed; they were all burst open and spoiled. Spoiled apparently; but it was not so; they were better than raw ones. Fire is beautiful; some day it will be useful, I think.

星期五

上星期一黄昏的时候，我又看见了他，但只有一会儿而已。我心里希望他会因我努力改善这里而表扬我，因为我一直很好心，又非常努力。可他并不高兴，转身离开了我。让他不高兴的另有原因：我再次劝说他，不要再到瀑布上去。

Friday

I saw him again, for a moment, last Monday at nightfall, but only for a moment. I was hoping he would praise me for trying to improve the estate, for I had meant well and had worked hard. But he was not pleased, and turned away and left me. He was also displeased on another account: I tried once more to persuade him to stop going over the Falls.

因为火让我懂得了一种新的强烈情感。它是全新的，显然不同于爱、悲伤以及我已经发现的那些情感，这种情感是恐惧。太可怕了！我希望我从来没有发现恐惧；它让我阴郁沮丧，它破坏了我的幸福，它让我战栗、发抖、心悸。但我无法说服他，因为他还没有发现恐惧，所以他不能理解我。

That was because the fire had revealed to me a new passion—quite new, and distinctly different from love, grief, and those others which I had already discovered—FEAR. And it is horrible!—I wish I had never discovered it; it gives me dark moments, it spoils my happiness, it makes me shiver and tremble and shudder. But I could not persuade him, for he has not discovered fear yet, and so he could not understand me.

亚当日记续

或许我该记着她还小，只是个小女孩，需要体贴。她兴趣盎然、充满渴望与活力。对她来说，这世界迷人、神奇、神秘又充满乐趣。当她发现一朵没见过的花，她会高兴得说不出话，她一定会拍拍它、摸摸它、闻闻它，还要跟它说说话，给它取上许多可爱的名字。

Perhaps I ought to remember that she is very young, a mere girl and make allowances. She is all interest, eagerness, vivacity, the world is to her a charm, a wonder, a mystery, a joy; she can't speak for delight when she finds a new flower, she must pet it and caress it and smell it and talk to it, and pour out endearing names upon it.

她热爱各种色彩：棕色的岩石，黄色的沙子，灰色的苔藓，绿色的树叶，蓝色的天空；还有破晓时分的珍珠色，山巅的紫色阴影，日落时分在暗红色海洋中漂浮的金色岛屿，于层层浮云中游走的清幽明月，如珠宝般在浩瀚宇宙中闪闪发光的星星——在我眼中这些东西毫无用处，然而对她来说，这些都是有颜色的和壮丽的，这便足够了，她为此爱得如痴如醉。

And she is color-mad: brown rocks, yellow sand, gray moss, green foliage, blue sky; the pearl of the dawn, the purple shadows on the mountains, the golden islands floating in crimson seas at sunset, the pallid moon sailing through the shredded cloud-rack, the star-jewels glittering in the wastes of space—none of them is of any practical value, so far as I can see, but because they have color and majesty, that is enough for her, and she loses her mind over them.

如果她能安静几分钟，那就会出现一种宁静的景象。这时候我想我是愿意看她的，我确定，因为我已经意识到她是个美丽的新造物——柔韧修长，丰满匀称，敏捷而又优雅。一次，她站在一块巨石上沐浴着阳光，白得像大理石一般，她把那年轻的头颅微微后仰，一只手遮在眼睛上方，看一只鸟儿从空中飞过，我当时心想，她真美。

If she could quiet down and keep still a couple minutes at a time, it would be a reposeful spectacle. In that case I think I could enjoy looking at her; indeed I am sure I could, for I am coming to realize that she is a quite remarkably comely creature—lithe, slender, trim, rounded, shapely, nimble, graceful; and once when she was standing marble-white and sun-drenched on a boulder, with her young head tilted back and her hand shading her eyes, watching the flight of a bird in the sky, I recognized that she was beautiful.

星期一中午

不知道这个星球上有没有她不感兴趣的东西，就算有，我也不知道。我对有些动物漠不关心，而她却不是。她对所有动物一视同仁，对它们都感兴趣，将它们都视若珍宝，欢迎每个新成员。

Monday Noon

If there is anything on the planet that she is not interested in it is not in my list. There are animals that I am indifferent to, but it is not so with her. She has no discrimination, she takes to all of them, she thinks they are all treasures, every new one is welcome.

当那头庞大的雷龙大步闯入我们的住处时，她把它看作意外收获的宝贝，我则认为它是场灾难。这说明我们对事物常常意见相左。她想驯化它，而我宁愿把家送给它，一走了之。

When the mighty brontosaurus came striding into camp, she regarded it as an acquisition, I considered it a calamity; that is a good sample of the lack of harmony that prevails in our views of things. She wanted to domesticate it, I wanted to make it a present of the homestead and move out.

她相信只要善待它，就可以驯服它，让它成为不错的宠物。我说，一头二十一英尺高、八十四英尺长的宠物，不适合养在这里，即使它毫无恶意，也会在无意中把我们的住处压垮。看看它的眼神就知道，它总是心不在焉。

She believed it could be tamed by kind treatment and would be a good pet; I said a pet twenty-one feet high and eighty-four feet long would be no proper thing to have about the place, because, even with the best intentions and without meaning any harm, it could sit down on the house and mash it, for any one could see by the look of its eye that it was absent-minded.

尽管如此，她仍然对驯服雷龙充满信心，不愿放弃。她打算用它来开一家乳品店，还希望我帮忙挤奶。但我才不干呢，这太冒险了。它的性别不对，我们也没有梯子。之后她又想骑着它看看风景。它的尾巴有三四十英尺长，拖在地上，就像一棵倒下的树，她以为可以顺着尾巴爬上去，但她想错了。当她一爬到陡峭的地方，就会很滑，她一下子跌倒了，要是没有我，她肯定会受伤。

Still, her heart was set upon having that monster, and she couldn't give it up. She thought we could start a dairy with it, and wanted me to help milk it; but I wouldn't; it was too risky. The sex wasn't right, and we hadn't any ladder anyway. Then she wanted to ride it, and look at the scenery. Thirty or forty feet of its tail was lying on the ground, like a fallen tree, and she thought she could climb it, but she was mistaken; when she got to the steep place it was too slick and down she came, and would have hurt herself but for me.

她现在满意了吗？没有。她觉得所有想法都要试验，否则就不可信。我承认这种精神是对的，而且这种精神很吸引我。我受到了她的影响，如果我和她在一起待得更久，我或许也会染上这种脾性。她对这庞然大物还剩一个想法去实践：她想，如果我们能驯服它，让它变得友善，我们就可以站在河里，让它给我们当桥用。

Was she satisfied now? No. Nothing ever satisfies her but demonstration; untested theories are not in her line, and she won't have them. It is the right spirit, I concede it; it attracts me; I feel the influence of it; if I were with her more I think I should take it up myself. Well, she had one theory remaining about this colossus: she thought that if we could tame it and make him friendly we could stand in the river and use him for a bridge.

事实证明，它已经足够温驯了，至少对她来说，的确如此——这样，她就开始实践，但是失败了：每次她把它领到河中央合适的位置后，自己回到岸边打算过桥，但每次它都会走上来，在她后面跟着，好像我们养了一座山当宠物。其他动物也一样，它们全都如此。

It turned out that he was already plenty tame enough—at least as far as she was concerned—so she tried her theory, but it failed: every time she got him properly placed in the river and went ashore to cross over him, he came out and followed her around like a pet mountain. Like the other animals. They all do that.

夏娃日记续

星期五

星期二、星期三、星期四和今天——我一直没见到他。因为独处的缘故，这段时间显得很长。不过，一个人待着总比不受待见好。

Friday

Tuesday—Wednesday—Thursday—and today: all without seeing him. It is a long time to be alone; still, it is better to be alone than unwelcome.

我得有人陪伴——我想我就是为此而生的——所以我和动物们交朋友。动物们真是迷人，它们性情温柔、温驯礼貌。

I HAD to have company—I was made for it, I think—so I made friends with the animals. They are just charming, and they have the kindest disposition and the politest ways.

它们从不闹脾气，也从不让你觉得自己是在冒犯它们。它们会笑着朝你摇尾巴（如果有的话），随时准备和你嬉戏、远足或随便跟你去什么地方。我觉得它们是完美的绅士。这些天我过得很开心，从不觉得孤独。

They never look sour, they never let you feel that you are intruding, they smile at you and wag their tail, if they've got one, and they are always ready for a romp or an excursion or anything you want to propose. I think they are perfect gentlemen. All these days we have had such good times, and it hasn't been lonesome for me, ever.

孤独！不，我应该算不上孤独。为什么呢，我周围总是有一大堆动物，有时它们占了四五英亩那么大的地方，数都数不过来——

Lonesome! No, I should say not. Why, there's always a swarm of them around—sometimes as much as four or five acres—

如果你站在中间的一块岩石上，眺望那无尽的、毛茸茸的动物群，就会发现一片亮丽又斑驳的色彩，在阳光的照耀下闪烁着光泽，还像涟漪一样起伏着，让你觉得眼前是一面湖泊，虽然你知道那并不是；欢快的鸟儿成群地来去，如同风暴，大片的翅翼挥动着，像是飓风；当阳光照在那一大片挥动的羽翼上，它们便会呈现出各种各样的颜色，像是燃烧起来了一样，刺得你眼睛都看不见。

---

you can't count them; and when you stand on a rock in the midst and look out over the furry expanse it is so mottled and splashed and gay with color and frisking sheen and sun-flash, and so rippled with stripes, that you might think it was a lake, only you know it isn't; and there's storms of sociable birds, and hurricanes of whirring wings; and when the sun strikes all that feathery commotion, you have a blazing up of all the colors you can think of, enough to put your eyes out.

我们去很远的地方旅行，我去过很多地方，差不多所有地方我都去过了吧。因此，我是第一个，也是唯一的旅行者。我们行进的场面十分壮观，任何地方都没有这样的景象。为了舒适，我会骑在老虎或豹子的身上，因为它们皮毛柔软，弧形的后背也适合我，而且它们还这么漂亮。但如果要走远路，或者要看风景，我就骑大象。它得用长鼻子把我举到它背上去，不过我可以自己下来。准备宿营的时候，它坐下，我就从它后面滑下来了。

We have made long excursions, and I have seen a great deal of the world; almost all of it, I think; and so I am the first traveler, and the only one. When we are on the march, it is an imposing sight—there's nothing like it anywhere. For comfort I ride a tiger or a leopard, because it is soft and has a round back that fits me, and because they are such pretty animals; but for long distance or for scenery I ride the elephant. He hoists me up with his trunk, but I can get off myself; when we are ready to camp, he sits and I slide down the back way.

鸟和动物互相友好，没有任何争执。它们彼此交谈，也都跟我说话，不过那肯定是另外一种语言，因为它们说的话，我一句也听不懂；但当我回答的时候，它们往往都能理解，尤其是狗和大象。我为此很羞愧。这说明它们比我更聪明，因此应该高我一等。我有些恼怒，因为我自己想当主要实验品——我不仅是想，也计划这么做。

The birds and animals are all friendly to each other, and there are no disputes about anything. They all talk, and they all talk to me, but it must be a foreign language, for I cannot make out a word they say; yet they often understand me when I talk back, particularly the dog and the elephant. It makes me ashamed. It shows that they are brighter than I am, for I want to be the principal Experiment myself—and I intend to be, too.

如今我已经学了些东西，也算是得到了教育，但最初并不是。我当时很无知，一开始，我一直没有观察到水往山上流的情况，因为我不够聪明，这曾让我感到气恼；不过现在我不在意了。

I have learned a number of things, and am educated, now, but I wasn't at first. I was ignorant at first. At first it used to vex me because, with all my watching, I was never smart enough to be around when the water was running uphill; but now I do not mind it.

我实验了很多次，现在终于知道，水从来不会往山上流，除非在黑暗中。我之所以知道水是在黑暗中往山上流的，是因为山上的池水从不干涸，如果水不是在晚上流回去的话，池水早就干了。我们最好通过实验来证明事物，然后才能算真正懂了；反之，如果只依靠猜测、假设和推断，就永远不会获得教育。

I have experimented and experimented until now I know it never does run uphill, except in the dark. I know it does in the dark, because the pool never goes dry, which it would, of course, if the water didn't come back in the night. It is best to prove things by actual experiment; then you KNOW whereas if you depend on guessing and supposing and conjecturing, you never get educated.

有些事情，你不可能发现；但单凭猜想、假定，你也绝对不会知道“你不可能发现”。你必须有耐心，不断实验，直到最后你真正弄明白你不可能发现。而且这样做你也会感到快乐——这会让这个世界变得趣味无穷。

Some things you CAN’T find out; but you will never know you can’t by guessing and supposing: no, you have to be patient and go on experimenting until you find out that you can’t find out. And it is delightful to have it that way, it makes the world so interesting.

要是真的没有什么东西可以去探究，那才枯燥无味。只要努力去探寻不明了的事物，即便没有结果，那探寻的过程也一样有趣，我甚至还觉得更加有趣呢。在我发现水的秘密前，这一直是我珍爱的宝物，但我明白之后，就不是了，那种兴奋的感觉没有了，我还觉得有些失落。

If there wasn't anything to find out, it would be dull. Even trying to find out and not finding out is just as interesting as trying to find out and finding out, and I don't know but more so. The secret of the water was a treasure until I GOT it; then the excitement all went away, and I recognized a sense of loss.

通过实验，我知道了木头、干树叶、羽毛和很多别的东西会浮在水面；因此，根据这些累积的证据，你就知道石头也会漂浮。不过你只能满足于知道，因为没有办法证明——目前还没有。但我以后会找到办法——到那时候，那种兴奋就会消失。

By experiment I know that wood swims, and dry leaves, and feathers, and plenty of other things; therefore by all that cumulative evidence you know that a rock will swim; but you have to put up with simply knowing it, for there isn't any way to prove it—up to now. But I shall find a way—then *that* excitement will go.

这让我难过，因为我会逐渐发现所有事情的原理，然后就再也不会感到兴奋了，可我是那么喜欢兴奋的感觉！有一天晚上，我因为想这事想得都无法入睡了。

Such things make me sad; because by and by when I have found out everything there won't be any more excitements, and I do love excitements so! The other night I couldn't sleep for thinking about it.

起初，我不知道自己生来是干什么的，但现在我想，我应该去探索这个奇妙世界的秘密，去寻找快乐，感谢造物主的安排。我还有许多东西需要学习——我也希望如此；如果我省着点儿慢慢寻找，不急于全部找出，这些有待发现的事物的秘密就能多持续几个星期吧，我希望如此。

At first I couldn't make out what I was made for, but now I think it was to search out the secrets of this wonderful world and be happy and thank the Giver of it all for devising it. I think there are many things to learn yet—I hope so; and by economizing and not hurrying too fast I think they will last weeks and weeks. I hope so.

如果你抛起一根羽毛，它会在空中飘走，然后消失不见；然后你向上扔一个土块，它却不会飘走，而是掉在了地上，每次都是这样。我试了一次又一次，结果都是一样的。为什么呢？毫无疑问，它并不是真的落下来了，但为什么看起来像是落下来了呢？我想，这是视觉上的幻觉。

When you cast up a feather it sails away on the air and goes out of sight; then you throw up a clod and it doesn't. It comes down, every time. I have tried it and tried it, and it is always so. I wonder why it is? Of course it DOESN' T come down, but why should it SEEM to? I suppose it is an optical illusion.

我的意思是，飘走的羽毛和落下的土块，两种现象中有一种是幻觉。我不知道究竟哪一种是幻象。也许是羽毛；也许是泥土；我无法证明究竟是哪个。我只能演示其中的一个是假的，然后让大家自行判断。

I mean, one of them is. I don't know which one. It may be the feather, it may be the clod; I can't prove which it is, I can only demonstrate that one or the other is a fake, and let a person take his choice.

通过观察，我发现星星不能永存。一些我所见过的最美的星星融化了，从天空中落下来。既然一颗星星会融化，那所有的都可能融化；既然都有可能融化，就有可能都在同一天晚上融化。那时我一定会很难过。

By watching, I know that the stars are not going to last. I have seen some of the best ones melt and run down the sky. Since one can melt, they can all melt; since they can all melt, they can all melt the same night. That sorrow will come—I know it.

我打算每天晚上都端坐着看星星，直到睡着为止。我要把那闪闪发亮的星空留在记忆里，这样的话，哪怕它们都慢慢地消失了，我还能通过想象，将那些可爱的星星复原到漆黑的夜空中，让它们再次在那里闪烁，透过我模糊的泪眼，它们的数量还能增加一倍。

I mean to sit up every night and look at them as long as I can keep awake; and I will impress those sparkling fields on my memory, so that by and by when they are taken away I can by my fancy restore those lovely myriads to the black sky and make them sparkle again, and double them by the blur of my tears.

失去伊甸园之后

每当回忆时，伊甸园就像是一场梦。那里很美，美得无与伦比，美得令人痴迷；而现在，伊甸园没有了，我以后再也见不到了。

After The Fall

When I look back, the Garden is a dream to me. It was beautiful, surpassingly beautiful, enchantingly beautiful; and now it is lost, and I shall not see it any more.

虽然失去了伊甸园，但我找到了他，我很满足。他全心全意地爱我；我用我充满激情的本性之中的一切力量去爱他，我认为这是我的青春和性别使然。如果我问自己为什么爱他，我发现我并不知道，也不想知道，所以我觉得这种爱不是出于推理和统计，不像对其他爬行生物和动物的爱。一定是这样的。

The Garden is lost, but I have found HIM, and am content. He loves me as well as he can; I love him with all the strength of my passionate nature, and this, I think, is proper to my youth and sex. If I ask myself why I love him, I find I do not know, and do not really much care to know; so I suppose that this kind of love is not a product of reasoning and statistics, like one's love for other reptiles and animals. I think that this must be so.

我爱某些鸟儿，是因为它们会唱歌；但我爱亚当，并不是因为他会唱歌——不，不是这样的。他唱得越多，我就越不能欣赏。可我还是让他唱，因为我希望去学着喜欢他感兴趣的一切。我确信我能做到，因为一开始我无法忍受，但现在已经习惯了。他一唱歌，牛奶都会发酸，但这没关系；哪怕是酸牛奶我也能适应。

I love certain birds because of their song; but I do not love Adam on account of his singing—no, it is not that; the more he sings the more I do not get reconciled to it. Yet I ask him to sing, because I wish to learn to like everything he is interested in. I am sure I can learn, because at first I could not stand it, but now I can. It sours the milk, but it doesn't matter; I can get used to that kind of milk.

我爱他，不是因为他的聪明——不，不是这样的。聪明程度——虽不很高——并不由他决定，因为那不是他自己创造的；连他自身也是上帝创造的，这够明白的了。我知道这其中蕴含着智慧。随着时间的推移，他的智慧也会日益发展，虽然我觉得这不会在一夜之间突然发生；不过不用急——他现在就很好。

It is not on account of his brightness that I love him—no, it is not that. He is not to blame for his brightness, such as it is, for he did not make it himself; he is as God make him, and that is sufficient. There was a wise purpose in it, THAT I know. In time it will develop, though I think it will not be sudden; and besides, there is no hurry; he is well enough just as he is.

我爱他，不是因为他的友善、体贴、周到。不是的，他在这方面有些欠缺，但他就这样也很好，而且他还在进步。

It is not on account of his gracious and considerate ways and his delicacy that I love him. No, he has lacks in this regard, but he is well enough just so, and is improving.

我爱他，不是因为他的勤奋——不，不是这样的。我知道他有勤奋的品质，但不明白他为什么要藏起这个优点来，不让我知道。这是我唯一的苦恼。除此之外，他对我都很坦诚。我相信，除了这一点，他对我没有任何隐瞒。

It is not on account of his industry that I love him—no, it is not that. I think he has it in him, and I do not know why he conceals it from me. It is my only pain. Otherwise he is frank and open with me, now. I am sure he keeps nothing from me but this.

不过，他有秘密不告诉我让我很伤心，有时候我想着这件事，会睡不着觉，但我会把这个念头从脑子中赶走。这不会破坏我的快乐，总的来说，我心中充满快乐，要不是因为他不告诉我秘密，满得都要溢出来了。

It grieves me that he should have a secret from me, and sometimes it spoils my sleep, thinking of it, but I will put it out of my mind; it shall not trouble my happiness, which is otherwise full to overflowing.

我爱他，不是因为他所受的教育——不，不是这样的。他是自学的，他的确也知道很多事情，但事情实际上并不是那样的。

It is not on account of his education that I love him—no, it is not that. He is self-educated, and does really know a multitude of things, but they are not so.

我爱他，不是因为他的勇敢——不，不是这样的。他告发了我，但我不怪他。我觉得这是他的性别特点，而他的性别不是他造就的。当然，我就不会告发他，那样我还不如先去死；但这也是性别的特点吧，我也不认为这是我的功劳，毕竟我的性别也不是我造就的。

It is not on account of his chivalry that I love him—no, it is not that. He told on me, but I do not blame him; it is a peculiarity of sex, I think, and he did not make his sex. Of course I would not have told on him, I would have perished first; but that is a peculiarity of sex, too, and I do not take credit for it, for I did not make my sex.

那么我为什么爱他呢？我想，只是因为他是男性吧。

他本质上很善良，我爱他这一点，但如果没有这一点，我依旧会爱他。就算他打我，虐待我，我也会继续爱他。我知道我会这样。我认为这是性别的问题。

Then why is it that I love him? MERELY BECAUSE HE IS MASCULINE, I think.

At bottom he is good, and I love him for that, but I could love him without it. If he should beat me and abuse me, I should go on loving him. I know it. It is a matter of sex, I think.

他强壮又英俊，我因此而爱他，我欣赏他，为他感到骄傲，但如果他没有这些品质，我也会爱他。如果他相貌平凡，我会爱他；如果他身体病弱，我也会爱他；我会替他干活，伺候他，为他祈祷，守候在他的床边，直到我死去。

He is strong and handsome, and I love him for that, and I admire him and am proud of him, but I could love him without those qualities. If he were plain, I should love him; if he were a wreck, I should love him; and I would work for him, and slave over him, and pray for him, and watch by his bedside until I died.

是的。我想，我爱他只因为他是我的，而且他是男性。我觉得没有别的原因。所以，正如我一开始说的那样：这种爱不是出于推理和统计。爱就这样降临了——谁也不知道它来自何处——无法解释，也无须解释。

Yes, I think I love him merely because he is MINE and is MASCULINE. There is no other reason, I suppose. And so I think it is as I first said: that this kind of love is not a product of reasonings and statistics. It just COMES—none knows whence—and cannot explain itself. And doesn't need to.

这就是我的想法。不过，我只是个女孩，又是第一个思考这个问题的女孩，也很有可能因为我有些无知又缺乏经验，我所想的这些都不对。

It is what I think. But I am only a girl, the first that has examined this matter, and it may turn out that in my ignorance and inexperience I have not got it right.

四十年后

我祈祷，我渴望，我希望我们两人能一起结束这一生——这种渴望永远不会从世界上消失，它会永存于每一个深爱丈夫的妻子心中，直到地老天荒；并且它将以我的名字命名。

Forty Years Later

It is my prayer, it is my longing, that we may pass from this life together—a longing which shall never perish from the earth, but shall have place in the heart of every wife that loves, until the end of time; and it shall be called by my name.

可是，如果我们中有一个必须先离世，我祈祷那个人会是我；因为他强大，我脆弱，我对他来说并不像他对我那样重要——没有他，我的生活就不完整。那我怎么能受得了？这祈祷也是不朽的，只要我的种族延续，它就不会停止。我是人类的第一位妻子，而人类最后一位妻子也会这样做。

But if one of us must go first, it is my prayer that it shall be I; for he is strong, I am weak, I am not so necessary to him as he is to me—life without him would not be life; how could I endure it? This prayer is also immortal, and will not cease from being offered up while my race continues. I am the first wife; and in the last wife I shall be repeated.

在夏娃墓前

亚当言：

她在哪里，

哪里就是伊甸园。

At Eve's Grave

ADAM:

Wheresoever she was,

THERE was Eden.

图书在版编目（CIP）数据

亚当夏娃日记：汉英对照 /（美）马克·吐温（Mark Twain）著；徐彬，张怡青译．—南京：译林出版社，2024.7

书名原文：Diaries of Adam and Eve
ISBN 978-7-5753-0111-4

I.①亚… II.①马… ②徐… ③张… III.①英语－汉语－对照读物 IV.①H319.4

中国国家版本馆 CIP 数据核字（2024）第 072621 号

亚当夏娃日记 〔美国〕马克·吐温 / 著 徐 彬 张怡青 / 译

责任编辑 陈绍敏
特约编辑 杨红丹 苏雪莹
装帧设计 鹏飞艺术
校　　对 刘文硕
责任印制 贺 伟

出版发行 译林出版社
地　　址 南京市湖南路 1 号 A 楼
邮　　箱 yilin@yilin.com
网　　址 www.yilin.com
市场热线 010-85376701
排　　版 鹏飞艺术
印　　刷 北京天恒嘉业印刷有限公司
开　　本 787 毫米 ×1092 毫米 1/32
印　　张 7.5
版　　次 2024 年 7 月第 1 版
印　　次 2024 年 7 月第 1 次印刷
书　　号 ISBN 978-7-5753-0111-4
定　　价 42.80元